FOOTBALL THE BASICS

National Library of Canada Cataloguing in Publication

Schaeffer, Jeffrey W., 1971-
        Football, the basics : strategies and techniques / Jeffrey W.
Schaeffer.

ISBN 1-4120-0512-4

        I. Title.

GV953.5.S33 2003   796.332'2   C2003-903386-4

TRAFFORD

This book was published *on-demand* in cooperation with Trafford Publishing. On-demand publishing is a unique process and service of making a book available for retail sale to the public taking advantage of on-demand manufacturing and Internet marketing. **On-demand publishing** includes promotions, retail sales, manufacturing, order fulfilment, accounting and collecting royalties on behalf of the author.

Suite 6E, 2333 Government St., Victoria, B.C. V8T 4P4, CANADA

Phone	250-383-6864	Toll-free	1-888-232-4444 (Canada & US)
Fax	250-383-6804	E-mail	sales@trafford.com
Web site	www.trafford.com	TRAFFORD PUBLISHING IS A DIVISION OF TRAFFORD HOLDINGS LTD.	
Trafford Catalogue #03-0881		www.trafford.com/robots/03-0881.html	

10   9   8   7   6   5   4   3

FOOTBALL THE

BASICS

STRATEGIES AND TECHNIQUES

By

Jeffrey W. Schaeffer

This book is dedicated to the memory of my mother Elizabeth M. Kraft. For her unconditional love and support of my brother and I. She worked hard as a single parent to support and raise us. She finally lost her struggle with Multiple Sclerosis (MS) on Thanks Giving day 1997. She was hard working, true, courageous, moral, and just. She was an amazing woman and I miss her immensely.

About the Author

1. 6 May 2000 Methodist College, Fayetteville NC. B.S. Business Administration, Concentration in Health Care Administration.

2. 1987 All County 1st team football, Lebanon County Pennsylvania. Eastern Lebanon County H.S. 11th grade.
   Linebacker- 99 tackles in 9 games. 11 tackles-per-game avg.

3. 1988 and 1991 United States Powerlifting Federation (USPF), Pennsylvania State Teenage Powerlifting Champion. 165 lb. class and 181 lb. class. 1990 Second place finish.

4. 1990 American Powerlifting Association (APA), Teenage National Champion, Powerlifting, 181 lb. class.

5. 4 Time: World Powerlifting Alliance (WPA), Teenage World Record Holder. 181 lb. class.

6. 1991- 1996 Paratrooper: US Army, 82nd Airborne Division. Martial Arts training: Shotokan karate, Sil Lum Kung Fu, and Jujitsu.

7. 1996- 1999 Methodist College Football, Fullback #36.
   4 year letterman, 2 year starter. Strongest athlete on the team.

8. 2001 Norfolk Nighthawks, Arena Football 2 League.
   Players contract signed, Fullback/Linebacker position.

Contents

CHAPTER ONE

THE BEGINNING

Chapter 1: The beginning

I spent all of my youth growing up in a suburb of Reading Pennsylvania. It was the typical working class, factory and steel town. Tough, fast-paced, and exciting, with the ability to step into nature and find yourself fishing along the Schuylkill river, the Tulpehocken creek, or the Blue Marsh lake.

I don't remember at what age I first started to play sports, but as far back as I can remember I was doing just that. My youth was a great time in my life. Numerous hours of the day were taken up by playing sports, and whatever sport was in season at that time we played. If it was football season then we played football. If it was hockey season then we played hockey. And if it was baseball season then we played baseball.

For most of this stage of my life we lived in Douglassville Pennsylvania. My mother married Thomas Kraft. Tom was a half Italian/ half German man from Phoenixville PA. He poured molten steel in a steel foundry for probably twenty years until a few years ago when he retired and moved to the mountains of Idaho. It was hard and dangerous work, but he loved it. I can still remember the holes burned one half inch deep, in his legs, from molten steel splashing down behind his protective leggings.

The start of my football career came in the form of mights' and midgets' football. One evening my parents asked my older brother Jason and I if we wanted to play Might's football. We instantly said yes. So the following evening we went to sign up with the Amity Vikings. They issued us all the battle gear required for full contact football. I never had to use this kind of armor before so I didn't know what was about to happen. The next evening we went to the first practice. The first thing that happened was that we suited up, and then we were evaluated for positions. And wouldn't you know that I was placed five yards across from a line of four kids with my brother Jason in front. It was the one on one drill. I was wearing full battle gear and I was going up against my older brother. This couldn't be good, because to my older brother I was a punching bag and a toy made to experiment on. I'm sure that other younger brothers can relate to this. Then the coach handed me the football and instructed me to run when the whistle was blown. This was just great; I was going to have to run for my life in a cruel game of smear the short kid. Now I was that small hyper kid who couldn't stand still and I ran like a jackrabbit. Fearing for my life when the whistle blew, I took off ducking and weaving in all directions. My brother completely missed me so the coach started sending the other kids one at a time. I dodged them all. Then there went my brother with miss number two. I was running the gauntlet and I didn't want to get killed. Finally on his third attempt my brother shoe-string tackled me, and to my amazement it didn't hurt. That ended my fear for the rest of mights' and midgets' football. I probably ran the equivalent of fifty yards ducking and weaving, and Jason finally tackled me five yards down field. I ran in every direction except down field. And to this day I still laugh when I think about it.

Mights' and Midgets' football was so much fun. We played games on sunny days, in the rain, and in a foot of snow. Football was a blast and I was hooked. I already knew that I was going to play college football, as would my brother Jason.

I remember one game in particular when I caught two interceptions. I was playing a modified outside linebacker. The offense lined up in a funny way early in the game. The quarterback took the snap and immediately turned towards me. He passed the football to the receiver that I was in front of. I tackled him. Later in the first half the offense lined up in the same way. I couldn't believe it; they were going to try the same play on me again. This time as soon as the quarterback turned and threw the football, I broke straight down field and jumped as high as I could. I caught the football over my head and sprinted down field toward the end zone. I was shorter than every one else and the receiver caught me from behind and tackled me on the five-yard line. My parents said that I took two steps for each one of his steps. I was so close to scoring a touchdown. I didn't know it back then, but I was already reading formations, the quarterback, and the angle and trajectory of the football in flight. It was now late in the game and, wouldn't you know it, the offense lined up the same way again.

The Beginning

Here it was that same play again. This time I was determined to score a touchdown. So when the quarterback took the snap and turned to throw the football, I broke straight down field. I jumped as high as I could and caught the football over my head. Then I sprinted straight down field as hard as I could. I could taste the end zone but, that same receiver caught me from behind and tackled me. This time it was on the one-yard line. I was so close, but that's the game of football, unpredictable and exciting. I loved it.

The next stage of my football career came in the form of high school football. It was just as exciting as Might's and Midgets' football, but slightly more competitive. We practiced the basic principals and techniques. It was at this stage in my carrier that I realized my ability to perform knock-down lead blocks. I started at both the fullback and the strong side linebacker positions. It was also during this stage in my carrier that I discovered my ability to effectively pursue and tackle ball carriers. I was already running the 40 yard dash in the high 4.5s to low 4.6 seconds. As a result I was named to the All County 1st team for football, Lebanon County PA, at the linebacker position. Playing both ways that season, I achieved 99 tackles at the linebacker position and over 400 yards rushing at the fullback position and, I did it in 9 games. This was because I missed a game due to an injury.

After high school I put off college to go into the army. I enlisted during the gulf war after seeing footage of a group of paratroopers, from the 82nd Airborne Division, hooting and hollering at the cameras. They were fired up, with their mouths opened, holding up their index fingers in a sign of we're number one. You could feel the energy through that television. It was strange, but at that moment I knew that I was going to be one of them. I knew that the next stage of my life would be as a paratrooper in the famed 82nd Airborne Division. After initial training I spent four years on Ft. Bragg in the "Double A", "Eighty Duce". That period of my life changed me from a snotty kid to a mentally tough man. This was the main reason that I was able to succeed in the classroom, on the football field, and in life. I will forever be an old paratrooper. It is a part of me, from the way I walk, to the way I think and react in all situations. I am and always will be proud of that. Huuaa!

Figure 1B I smile before a good "Hollywood" jump from a C47 aircraft.

Figure 1C I jump on a pass from a C130 aircraft.

In March of 1996 my enlistment was up and it was time to go back to playing football. I was now ready to pursue a college education and the college gridiron. Being married at the time I looked for a school that was close to my house. I needed to be able to drive to school, attend classes and practice, drive to work at Home Depot, and drive home. Methodist College was the answer. It was a small, private, liberal arts College with good academics and one-on-one interaction with the professors. The small class sizes were important to my ability to learn, while working 30 hours a week and playing football. Unfortunately during this stage of my life, my marriage to Carla had ended in divorce. There were a lot of opponents on the football field who got whooped, as a result of my releasing frustrations from that divorce.

College was a blast and playing college football was exhilarating. The energy and emotions of playing in a big game is incredible. It is an experience that is unforgettable and amazing. I can still recall the feeling of the energy, coming from the crowd and my teammates. It was electric. There were even times when the sideline referee would look back and smile, from the energy coming towards him. There were even referees who looked back and said, "this school spirit is incredible". Being a part of the energy and excitement of college football was probably why they refereed. College football was something that was always on my mind, even during my military days. It was even better than my expectations and well worth the wait.

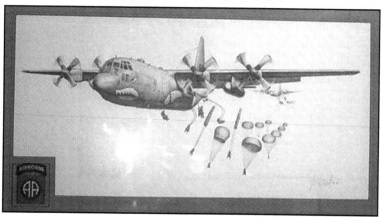

CHAPTER TWO

BALANCE

Chapter 2: Balance

By understanding how the body moves while staying in balance, a person will be able to use balance to his advantage in competitive sports. When a person moves he must stay in balance in order to avoid falling to the ground. So balance plays an important part in virtually all aspects of playing football. Thus it makes sense that if the player can understand this process, it will make him a better competitor. Finally, a player that has studied movement should be able to manipulate it to his advantage.

In numerous Martial Arts styles, different techniques are utilized to maintain balance during blocking, striking, entering, and evading movements. Figure 2A shows a person standing in the upright position. A vertical line is drawn through the middle of the person showing the "center line". The position of the person's feet (his base) in relation to his upper body will determine his balance point. In figure 2A the balance point is located on the centerline.

Figure 2B shows the person's upper body located to the right of his base and the centerline. In this position the person's balance point is now located to the right of the centerline and over his left leg. As a result the person is off balance, and could easily be forced to fall down to the ground, by pushing on the outside of

Figure 2A   **Figure 2B**

21

his right shoulder. You will see this principle being utilized in later chapters of this book for blocking and rushing techniques.

As long as a person keeps both of his feet at least shoulder width apart and planted on the ground, he will maintain a solid base. This will give him the best opportunity to fight off forces that are being placed against him. However, when he picks up one of his feet to step or move he will briefly loose the stability of a solid base. This will make it easier to control him by taking advantage of his weak point (i.e. the raised foot). That is why many martial arts styles slide their feet across the ground to move. You will see this principle being utilized in later chapters for pass rushing techniques.

When a person keeps his balance point on the centerline, he can run forward and backwards in the most efficient manner. Figure 2C shows the person in a good power position. You will notice that the player's head, shoulders, hips, knees, and feet are all aligned on the centerline. To take the person out of the power position, all that has to be done is to move one of the named body parts off of the centerline. Figure 2D shows the person being taken out of the power position by pushing his hips off of the centerline.

Figure 2C

Fig.2D

Balance

If you view the person from the side, standing in an upright position, you will also be able to see the centerline. Figure 2E demonstrates this principle. Now the person can be put off balance by pushing his shoulders backwards placing his upper body behind the centerline. Figure 2F demonstrates this principle. You will find this principal being utilized in the proper tackling technique described later in this book.

Figure 2E   **Figure 2F**

Balance is a subject that every football player should study and master. It will enable the player to perform at a higher level and, it will allow for a greater number of choices that the player can take advantage of during a play. Martial Arts training will develop higher levels of balance and an in-depth understanding of how it works. That's why every player should consider taking some form of Martial Arts training.

Proper body position will ensure that the player maintains good balance. This will allow him to react and move in the most efficient manner. And the basic forms are designed to utilize the best body position. Therefore, the basic forms should be practiced until they become instinctive. This means that the player will automatically get into the proper body position without thinking about it.

CHAPTER THREE

OFFENSIVE LINEMEN

The offensive linemen are the workhorses of the offensive squad. They are the first players that make contact with the defense. They are charged with the task of opening holes for the running backs and protecting the quarterback from the pass rush. And they must perform this job with skill and brute force.

An offensive lineman at the college level should be at least 6'1" tall and weigh at least 250 lbs. In my football career I have played with offensive linemen who were as big as 6'9" tall and weighed around 400 lbs. The offensive lineman must be strong, agile, and quick with the ability to move in all directions. Superior leg strength should be viewed as a necessity for the offensive lineman.

Proper Form

I cannot stress enough how important it is for the offensive lineman to utilize proper form and technique. This is because it will ensure that he maintains a solid base and a powerful body position. When the offensive lineman performs a pass blocking sequence, he will be moving backwards while the defender is moving forward. Because this gives the defender an obvious advantage, the offensive lineman must stay in a powerful position or he will risk being run over.

The first thing that the offensive lineman must learn is to take a proper power position. Start by standing in the upright position. Next, place your feet shoulder width apart or slightly wider than shoulder width apart. Your feet should point outward slightly to maintain the proper alignment of your knees and ankles. Now bend slightly at the knees and the waist to lower your center of gravity. Push your chest out slightly and bring your head up so that you have a clear field of view. Now put your hands out to the front with the palms facing outward and the fingers pointed upward. This is done to make contact with the defender. Figure 3A demonstrates the proper power position.

Figure 3A The power position

Starting Stances

There are two types of starting stances that are commonly used by the offensive lineman. They are the 2-point stance and the 3-point stance. The 2-point stance is commonly used for pass blocking because it allows the lineman to start moving backwards as fast as possible. However, when the offensive lineman is in a 2-point stance, it lets the defense know that the offensive line is probably going to pass block. The 3-point stance gives the offensive lineman a sprinting type starting position. This position lowers the lineman's center of gravity allowing him to explode forward off of the line of scrimmage. This start will give the lineman the driving force required to move a defender out of his running lane.

In order to utilize the 3-point stance, first get into the proper position on the line of scrimmage. Now take a proper stance as described earlier. Next lean down and place your right hand on the ground with just your fingertips touching the turf. Place your left hand on your left thigh in a comfortable position. Your feet can be staggered with one foot placed around 6 inches ahead of the other. Remember to place the opposite hand of the foot that is placed forward, down on the turf. Doing this gives you a sprinter's type starting position by simulating a natural running stride.

28

Staggering your feet will also allow you to rotate your hips easier, enabling you to pull for a crack block or trap block. Figure 3B demonstrates a proper 3-point stance. Figure 3C shows that placing one foot back will make it easier for you pull in that direction.

FIGURE 3C   PULLING

Figure 3B The 3-point stance

The 2-point stance is an easy technique to master. Start by getting into the proper position, on the line of scrimmage. Next take a proper stance. Stagger your feet by placing the outside foot back about 6 inches behind the inside foot. Now bend at the knees and waist to place you into a good power position. Keep your head up to see the defender in front of you. Finally place your hands on your upper thighs. Figure 3D demonstrates the 2-point stance.

Figure 3D The 2-point stance

The Pass Step

As I have discussed earlier, it is crucial for the offensive line-man to maintain a powerful body position while pass blocking. Leg strength will help him move while maintaining a good base and power position. The technique that the offensive lineman uses to move while pass blocking can be referred to as the "pass step".

To carry out the "pass step", start by taking a good 2-point stance. Now the pass step is made up of two foot-movements. To start moving bring your hands up and to the front with the palms facing out and fingers pointing upward. At the same time, to move to the left, take a step to the left with your lead or left foot. Then slide your right foot, just above the ground, to the left returning to the original starting position for your feet. You have just success-fully moved a foot or two to the left, while maintaining a solid base and a good power position. Figure 3E demonstrates the pass step technique. Remember the key is to always keep your feet at least shoulder width apart.

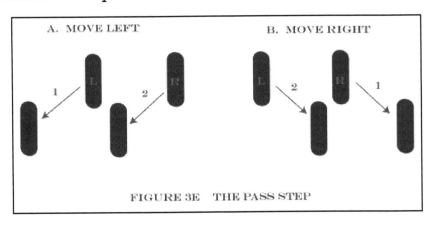

FIGURE 3E   THE PASS STEP

Cut Blocking

Cut blocking is a technique that can be utilized to bring the defender down to the ground, taking him out of the play. A cut block can be used on a running play and a delayed cut block can be used on a pass play. Pass plays are timed to allow the receiver to get to a certain position down field to defeat the defense. So a delayed cut block is designed to put the defender down on the ground, when the pass is delivered. This stops the defender from being able to block the pass.

To carry out an effective cut block, you need to do a few things well. Start by taking a good 3-point stance. Next drive off of the line of scrimmage. Now just before impact is made, with the defender, drop down and drive through his legs. Extend your arms forward around the defender's legs. This will help to trip him if he tries to step over you. You should essentially dive through his legs around 3 to 4 inches below his knees. Remember to keep your head up so that you can see the defender, and to keep your neck out of an injury prone position. The key thing to remember is to never, and I mean never, make contact with the top of your head. If the defender recovers then go to your hands and knees, close the distance by crawling forward, and dive through his legs again.

To carry out a delayed cut block, start in either a 2 or 3-point stance. Next, drive off of the line of scrimmage and make contact with the defender up high. Then, after a certain time period, say 2 seconds, drop down and dive through the defender's legs. Extend your arms forward around his legs to help to trip him. If the defender recovers go to your hands and knees, recoil, and dive through his legs again. Keep your head up so that you can see the defender, and to keep your neck out of an injury prone position. Remember that a delayed cut block cannot be used if another player is blocking the defender up high.

Blocking:

Blocking is the offensive linemen's main job and focus. His technique and skill will play a crucial role in his ability to carry out this function. His ability to overpower his opponent will also make him successful at blocking. So one can see how important it is for the offensive lineman to possess superior strength and use the power position.

One of the blocking techniques that the offensive lineman will utilize is the driving block. This type of block will be used mostly on running plays. The object of this type of block is to drive the defender back off of the line of scrimmage. And a good driving block will result in the defender being pushed out of the running lane, put down to the ground, and pinned until the play is over.

To perform a driving block, start by getting into the proper position on the line of scrimmage. Take a 3-point starting stance and identify the player that you are assigned to block. Then once the football is snapped, explode forward off of the line of scrimmage and close the gap on the targeted defender. Keep your center of gravity low and maintain a good power position. Use the upper part of your chest and the front of your face mask to initially make contact with the defender. Then thrust your arms forward in an attempt to push the defender's upper body back behind his hips and off of his centerline. This will be similar to the bench-pressing motion and it will take the defender out of his power position. Keep your legs driving forward through the impact for the same reason that a boxer punches through his target. Your fingers can be hooked under the front sides of the defender's shoulder pads, with your thumbs pointing upward. This will make it harder for the defender to get away from you. But you must keep your momentum going forward while using this hand technique. This is because if you hook onto the defender and then pull backward, you will be called for a holding penalty. Figure 3F demonstrates the driving block.

Figure 3F   I perform a driving block.

Blocking sequences:

There are a number of different types of blocking sequences that will be utilized by the offensive linemen. They include the reach block, the influence to block, the double team block, the seal block, the trap block, the cog block, and the double team block to the second level assignment. Each technique will be used for specific reasons in the scheme of the play. And one play can be designed with multiple combinations of these blocking sequences.

The "reach block" is exactly what it states. If the defender lines up offset to your right and you are assigned to block him to the left. You will have to get to his right side to block him in that direction. To accomplish this, start by stepping off of the line of scrimmage with your right foot. This first step should be to the right in an attempt to get to in front of the defender. Then make contact with the defender while maintaining a good power position. Finally, turn the defender to the left and drive him back in that direction.

The "influence to block" is basically an attempt to get the defender to step in a direction that will set up the actual block, which in many cases will be a seal block. To do this, the offensive lineman will first make a specific movement, in an attempt to get the defender to react and move in the desired direction. Finally, the defender will be blocked essentially cutting him off from being able to pursue the football.

The "seal block" is used to stop the defender from being able to get to the ball carrier. This is accomplished by placing your body in between the defender and the ball carrier. This will effectively wall off the defender, stopping him from being able to close the gap on the ball carrier. To do this, all the blocker has to do is to make contact with the defender up high and step to the side that the ball carrier is going to pass him on. The blocker should set up on a slight angle between the front and the side of the defender. This will stop the defender from being able to move forward or to that side. Any blocking sequence can turn into a seal block.

The "double team" block is a tool that can be used to combat a powerful defender. This block is a simple technique to understand and master. To perform this block, two offensive players will drive off of the ball and block the defender at the same time. On a running play your assignment may be to block the play side linebacker. In this situation, you may be asked to double team the defensive lineman that is in the running lane, to push him backwards. Then release the defensive lineman to your teammate and close the gap on your assigned linebacker. Finally, blocking the linebacker out of the play. This technique can be referred to as the "double team to the second level assignment".

Drills:

1. Pass step drill

Mark off 20 yards. Start off at a walking pace. Step to the right with your right or outside foot while extending your arms as if you are pushing into a defender's chest. Then step to the right with your left or inside foot, finishing with your feet slightly wider than shoulder width apart. Repeat for 20 yards. Perform this drill moving to the left, right, and backwards. Once you have mastered the technique you can increase your speed.

2. Hand drill (2 people)

Start by having 2 linemen stand facing each other. Now take a proper stance and place your hands on the defender's chest. The defender will swat your hands off of his chest. Immediately replace your hands on his chest. This drill will build hand and eye coordination.

3. Rushing drill (1 on 1)

First face the defender. Next both players will get into their starting positions. Then the defender rushes right and you block left. This drill will help you master the blocking technique. Do this to the right and to the left. Once you have mastered the technique, then practice with the defender rushing in any direction including changing directions. Remember practice and repetition will make you better.

4. Push pull drill

Start by taking a proper stance. Then have another player face you. Place your hands on the outside of his front numbers. Next the defender will grab you on top of both of your shoulders. Finally the defender will push and pull you, trying to throw you off balance to make you fall down to the ground. This drill will force you to stay in a good blocking position with a low center of gravity. It will also teach you how to shift your weight to counter the defender's momentum. Remember good technique will keep you on your feet.

CHAPTER FOUR

QUARTERBACKS

The quarterback is the leader of the offensive squad. He must be alert, agile, and intelligent. He must posses the ability to read the situation and quickly choose the best course of action to take. Vision is an essential aspect of the quarterback's tool bag. Without good vision the quarterback will not be able to deliver an accurate pass to the receiver. The quarterback must also posses a strong throwing arm. And a taller quarterback will be able to see above and beyond the tall linemen of today.

Throwing The Football

To throw the football properly the quarterback must use proper technique as well as arm strength. Start by gripping the football with your throwing hand. Your fingers should be spread apart with the fingertips touching the football's laces. There should be a slight space between the palm of your hand and the football. Now place your opposite hand on the other side of the football. You can refer to this position as the "Ready Position". The ready position should be used when the quarterback is performing drop steps or setting up to pass the football. In this position the quarterback keeps both of his hands on the football. This will maximize his ability to hold onto the football in the event that a defender makes contact with him. Figure 4A demonstrates the Ready Position.

Figure 4A The Ready Position

Throwing the football from the ready position is a simple process. Start by setting your feet by planting them firmly on the ground, around shoulder width apart. Next check your receivers to identify your target. Then rotate your throwing arm straight back with your elbow bent at a 90-degree angle. The palm of your throwing hand should be facing forward. The opposite arm should point forward with the shoulder aiming at the target. Now rotate your throwing arm forward over the top of your shoulder. The elbow should lead your hand and be pulled down toward your side. At the same time pull your non-throwing arm down to your side. This motion will torque your upper body, transferring power to the football. Step toward the target with your lead foot. Release the football by allowing it to leave your hand. The ball will spin off of your fingers. So by flicking your fingers slightly you can control how the football spirals in flight. Your throwing hand should finish up pointing towards the target with the thumb facing down. Figure 4B demonstrates the throwing technique.

Figure 4B   The throwing technique

Hand Offs:

Using proper technique when handing off the football will reduce the risk of fumbling it. Hand offs can be carried out with either one or two hands. The two handed hand off can be accomplished easily from the ready position. First the quarterback takes the snap from the center. To hand off the football to either side, he will then simply rotate to that side and run back to the hand off point. As he passes the running back he simply lowers the football to that side and places it in the pocket between the runner's arms. After the hand off is complete, the quarterback returns his hands to the ready position and continues running carrying out a fake. Figure 4C demonstrates the two handed handoff.

Figure 4C   The Two handed handoff

Handing off the football using one hand increases the risk of a fumble. But using one hand can increase the speed of the handoff. This will make it harder for the defenders to see who has the football. This will also make a fake more effective. To hand off the football with one hand, start by taking the snap from the center. Next, rotate to the appropriate side and run back to the hand off point. Then as you pass the runner simply place the football into the pocket between his arms with one hand. Remember to use the hand on the same side that runner passes you on. Finally return your hand to the ready position and carry out a rollout. Figure 4D demonstrates the one handed hand off.

Figure 4D   The One Handed Hand off

Most offensive plays are designed to set up another play. A running play will force the defense to step up into the lane to stop the runner's forward progress. So the play action pass is designed to look like the running play, but then it turns into a pass. This may catch the defense playing the run and burn them with the pass. For this to work, the same amount of effort must be applied to the run and the run fake.

The difference between the run and the run fake is subtle. On the running play the quarterback places the football into the runner's pocket and releases it. But on the play action pass the quarterback places the football into or near the runner's pocket and then pulls it back to the ready position. He then rolls out holding the football close to his body to hide it from the defender's view. Finally, he will pull up and pass the football to the targeted receiver.

Pitching the Football:

There are two types of pitches that are used in different situations. They are the One-handed pitch or shovel pass and the Two-handed pitch or underhand pitch. The One-handed pitch is used while running, especially on the option play. And the Two-hand ed pitch is used to quickly pitch the football, particularly on a sweep play. Both techniques are easy to master.

To perform the underhand pitch or two-handed pitch, start by taking the snap from the center. Next pivot on the foot that is on the opposite side of the direction of the sweep play. This will turn you to the play side to face the pitch point. You will rotate about 120 degrees to the pitch point. With an underhand motion, rotate the football out and up toward the target. Release the football and frame the target with both hands. Finally return your hands to the ready position and carry out a rollout in the opposite direction of the play. Figure 4E demonstrates the two-handed pitch. The two-handed pitch can also be performed by pivoting on the foot that is on the same side of the direction of the sweep play. This will initially turn you away from the direction of the play. To do this you will have to rotate about 220 degrees to face the pitch point. Then pitch the football with both hands and continue by carrying out a rollout in the opposite direction. This version will briefly place the football out of the defense's field of view. Therefore, the play action pass version of this play will be more effective. Figure 4F demonstrates this version of the two-handed pitch.

Figure 4E   The Two-handed pitch
(Turning to play side)

Figure 4F   The Two-handed pitch
(Turning opposite to play side)

The one-handed pitch is a fairly simple technique to perform. Start by identifying the target receiver. Then from the ready position, rotate the football straight towards the receiver with your pitching hand. Release the football and frame the target with your hand pointing forward and your knuckles facing upward. Figure 4G demonstrates the one-handed pitch.

Figure 4G   The One-handed pitch

The Drop Step:

The drop-step consists of the quarterback taking crossover steps back from the line of scrimmage. This is done to give the primary receiver time to run his pass route. So in many cases the length of the pass route will reflect the number of drop steps taken by the quarterback. Common sequences of drop steps used are three, five, and seven step drop-steps. A three-step drop will be used for a short pass, for example, five yards. A five-step drop will be used for mid-range passes, for example, ten yards. And the seven-step drop will be used on a long pass, for example, the Hitch and Go.

To perform the drop step, start by taking the snap from the center. Next with the football in the ready position, turn to your throwing arm side and take the designated number of cross over steps back from the line of scrimmage. Then stop and set your feet while checking if your receivers are open. Finally, choose your target and deliver the football using the proper throwing technique. A key thing to remember is to look straight down field during your drop steps. This is done to make it harder for the defense to read which receiver you are going to throw the football to. Figure 4H demonstrates the 5-step drop step.

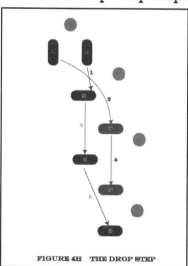

FIGURE 4H   THE DROP STEP

Drills:

1. "The Kneeling Pass":

This drill will help the quarterback develop proper form and technique. To perform this drill start with two players facing each other around five to ten yards apart. Both players will kneel down on the ground facing each other. One player will now take the football from the ready position and bring it back behind him using the throwing technique described earlier. Kneeling on the ground forces the player to rotate his torso. This will generate power that will be transferred to the football. Now the person will finish by throwing the football to the other player. They will continue to throw the football back and fourth for a set time period. Remember the players should always warm up and stretch before they throw the football hard. This will help them avoid injuring their throwing arms.

2. "The Trash Can or Barrel Pass":

This drill will help you develop accuracy and control in throwing the football. Start by taking a standard size trashcan and place it upright at different distances from you. Then practice throwing the football into the trash can at each distance. Remember the more that you throw the football the better your accuracy will become.

3. Pass Routes:

Now you can begin throwing pass routes with a receiver. Pass routes are an important part of practice because they will help you to develop your timing. The repetition of performing the pass route will also help you to gel with the receiver. Start with both the quarterback and the receiver lining up on the line of scrimmage. Then on the quarterbacks signal the snap is simulated. The quarterback will then take his designated number of drop steps. He will then stop, set his feet, and deliver the pass to the receiver. The goal is to deliver the pass at the right time to increase the effectiveness of the pass route.

Types of pass routes:

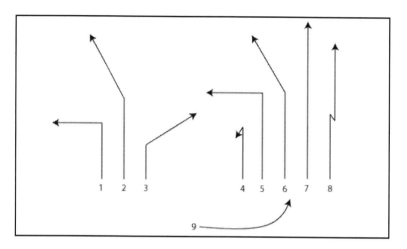

1. Five-n-out/ flat 2. Flag out 3. Cross 4. Five and Stop 5. Seam in 6. Post in 7. Fly/ Go 8. Hitch and Go 9. Swing

CHAPTER FIVE

RUNNING BACKS

Chapter 5: Running backs

The running back is a highly visible position. Generally there are three types of running backs, they are the "fullback", the "halfback", and the "tailback". First a team needs a big, strong running back that can block well and run defenders over for short yardage conversions. This type of running back is known as the fullback or blocking back. At the college level he should weigh somewhere between 235 pounds and 260 pounds. Second a team needs an agile running back with excellent speed to turn the corners on sweep plays. And he must also have good hands for catching passes. At the college level he should weigh somewhere between 190 pounds and 220 pounds. This type of running back is known as the tailback. The third type of running back is known as the halfback or all-purpose back. He is a medium sized running back who should have good speed. And he must be able to run the ball, catch the ball, and block well. He will weigh somewhere between 215 pounds to 230 pounds.

In my football career, I fell into the category of the halfback. But I played the fullback position at Methodist College. I was 5' 10" tall and I weighed 215 pounds. I ran the 40-yard dash in 4.3 seconds. I could both run the ball and catch the ball well, but I had superior strength and I was an excellent blocker. And my leg strength allowed me to excel at short yardage conversions. So I was utilized in lead blocking at the full back position.

Form:

There are two starting stances that are utilized by running backs. They are the "two-point stance" and the "three-point stance". The fullback will usually use the three-point starting stance except when he is offset to the right or the left. And the halfback and tailback will use the two-point starting stance.

To use the two-point starting stance, first take your position behind the quarterback. This will usually be seven yards back behind the line of scrimmage. Next place your feet around shoulder width apart. Then bend slightly at the knees and waist and place your hands on your upper thighs. Keep your head up to give you a better field of view. Now if you are initially moving to the right, then step off with the right foot. If to the left, then step off with the left foot. Remember that at an advanced level you will use a number of starting step sequences, but to step off with the foot that is on the same side that you are initially moving to is a good basic skill to have. Figure 5A demonstrates the two-point starting stance.

Figure 5A   The "2-point" stance

To use the three-point starting stance, first take your position behind the quarterback. For the fullback this will usually be five yards back from the line of scrimmage. Next place your feet around shoulder width apart. Then bend down and place you forearms on your thighs. Now rotate your comfortable arm down and forward placing your fingertips on the turf slightly ahead of your shoulder. Keep your head up so that you can see the football being snapped and where the defense is aligned. Remember to look at the football and always use your peripheral vision to observe the defense. This is done to ensure that you do not reveal where you are going. The back heels of your feet should be slightly up off of ground. This will allow you to explode out of your stance easier. Now explode out of your stance by stepping off with your right foot, to go to the right. Or step off with the left foot to go to the left. Figure 5B demonstrates the three-point starting stance.

Figure 5B   The "3-point" starting stance

Hand Offs:

"Hand offs" are fairly simple procedures to master. It is important to use proper technique when taking a hand off because it reduces the chance of fumbling the football. And as a running back you should strive to never give up the football. Remember, no fumbles!

To take a hand off from the quarterback, start by exploding out of your starting stance. Next run to the hand off point. If you are running to the right side of the quarterback then place your left arm across your chest. The elbow should be bent with the palm of the hand facing down. Place your right arm across your belly button with the elbow bent and the palm of your hand facing up. This technique creates a pocket between your arms where the quarterback can place the football. So once you feel the quarterback place the football into the pocket, then close your arms down onto it and grip it with your hands. From this position the football can be tucked away into one arm to allow you run at a full sprint. Remember that during contact with a defender, if you keep two hands on the football, you will reduce the chance of fumbling it. Also, keep in mind that whichever side the hand off comes from, the arm on that side will be placed across the chest. Figure 5C demonstrates the hand off position.

Figure 5C   The hand off position

Catching the football:

Catching the football is a skill that can be mastered with practice. Using proper technique to catch will increase the running back's effectiveness thus making him a threat to the defense. The running back should take pride in his ability to catch the football. It is better to catch the football with your hands, than it is to trap it against your body. This is because it reduces the chance of the football bouncing off of your body.

To catch the football properly, start by placing your hands out in front of your body. The palms of your hands will face forward. Now bend your elbows slightly and touch the tips of your index fingers and thumbs together. This creates a triangular space between your hands. And this is where the leading tip of the football is caught. Once the football enters your hands, squeeze down on the fat center part of it. Then tuck the football away and run down field towards the end zone. A key thing to remember is to "look the football into your hands", tuck it away, and then look down field for a running lane. If you take your eyes off of the football, before it is caught, you will probably miss it. Remember concentration is vital to succeeding at this technique. Figure 5D demonstrates proper catching technique.

Figure 5D   The catching position

To catch the football over your shoulder, start by placing your hands out to the front with the palms facing up. Bend your elbows slightly, and place the inside edges of your hands and pinkie fingers together. This creates a pocket in your hands to catch the football in. Look back over your shoulder to locate the football in flight and "look it into your hands". When the football enters your hands, squeeze down on the fat center part of it. The leading tip of the football will usually be caught in the fingers. Then tuck the football away and run down field towards the end zone. Extending your arms forward will telegraph the catch, so wait until the last second to do so. This technique will be utilized when sprinting down field towards the end zone, especially on a fly route. Figure 5E demonstrates catching over the shoulder.

Figure 5E   Catching over the shoulder

55

Blocking:

Blocking is a crucial aspect of playing the running back position. Strength and proper technique are both requirements for blocking well. These attributes can be developed through strength training and practicing good techniques. Once again the running back should strive to be an exceptional blocker.

Lead blocking is a vital part of many running plays. To carry out a good lead block, you must do a few things well. First, you must find the best line of travel to the defender that you are going to block. Next, explode out of your starting stance and close the gap to the defender, while building up speed. Now in the same way that a boxer punches through his target, you must explode through the defender, (not into the defender). This will help put the defender down on the ground where he cannot make a play on the ball carrier. Keep your head up so that you can see the defender and to keep your neck out of an injury prone position. Never make contact with the top of your head. Hit the defender on his front numbers with your facemask and the front of your shoulders. Continue driving your legs well past the point of impact. If you do this well you will excel at lead blocking. Fig. 5F demonstrates the lead block.

Figure 5F   I perform a knock down lead block.

Cut Blocking:

The "Cut block" is useful tool to have in your tool bag. The cut block can be used to bring a defender down to the ground, taking him out of the play. There are many situations where a cut block will be designed into a play. For example, a pass play can be designed in which the quarterback rolls out to the strong side of the field. So the defensive end will be cut down to the ground, by the fullback, to seal the corner for the quarterback.

To carry out a successful cut block, you need to do a few things well. First, you need to find the best line of travel to the defender that you are going to cut. Then explode out of your starting position and close the gap on the targeted defender. Build up your speed to the point of impact. Do this in the same manner that you would to carry out a lead block. This will ensure that the defender will not read that he is going to be cut until it is too late. Remember "don't telegraph the cut". The defender should accelerate towards you to take on the block. This will make the cut more effective by using the defender's momentum against him. Now just before the impact is made, with the defender, drop down and dive through his legs taking them out from under him. Aim for around 3 to 4 inches below his knees. Keep your head up so that you can see the defender and to keep your neck out of an injury prone position. Never make contact with the top of your head. Extend your arms forward around the outside of the defenders legs. This will help to trip him if he tries to step over you. If the defender recovers then go to your hands and knees, crawl forward, and dive through his legs again. Figure 5G demonstrates the cut block.

Figure 5G I perform a cut block.

Going in Motion:

Certain plays will require the running back to go in motion. This is done to confuse the defense and to place the running back in position to set up a play. Going in motion is a fairly simple thing to do. The motion will be cued by the quarterback with either a body gesture or a word in the snap count. You can either shuffle side ways or run side ways. A key thing to remember is that you must stay parallel to the line of scrimmage until the ball is snapped. Also, keep in mind that the rules will vary depending on the league you are playing in. So always become familiar with the rules of the game for the level that you are playing at. Figure 5H demonstrates how to go in motion parallel to the line of scrimmage.

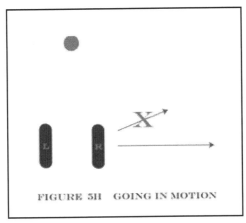

FIGURE 5H   GOING IN MOTION

Avoiding the Tackle:

The main goal of the offense is to get into the end zone to score a touch down. This means that the top priority of the running back is to get into the end zone carrying the football. Knowing this it is safe to say that, although it is fun to run over the defender, this increases the chance of being tackled. So this brings us to the topic of avoiding the tackle. Some of the best running backs of all time were masters of movement. They could cut, spin, stop and change direction, use speed bursts, and use hand plants to stay up off of the ground. A running back should work hard on mastering these techniques. This is because these techniques will make him unpredictable and harder to stop.

Cutting:

Cutting requires leg strength, agility, and good technique. The running back can cut by using two techniques. They are to cut off of the outside foot and to cut off of the inside foot. Both techniques are easy to perform.

To cut off of the outside foot, start by running down field. To cut to the left plant your right foot and step to the left with your left foot. Cutting in this way, while running hard, requires exceptional leg strength. If you are going to cut using this technique, I have found that it is best to keep your center of gravity low to the ground. Then right before you cut, make your feet lighter by reducing your momentum. This technique is a quick movement that changes your running angle. Figure 5I demonstrates cutting off of the outside foot.

When I used this technique, I would run straight at the defender to make him commit to the impact. Then just before the impact, I would cut to one side or the other. Because of my leg strength I would usually run through the impact and avoid the tackle. This is because when I cut, it placed the impact to the side of my centerline.

To cut off of the inside foot, start by running in one direction. Next briefly plant both of your feet on the ground. To cut to the left, take a cross over step with your right foot. Then step to the left, with your left foot, and continue running in that direction. Figure 5J demonstrates this technique.

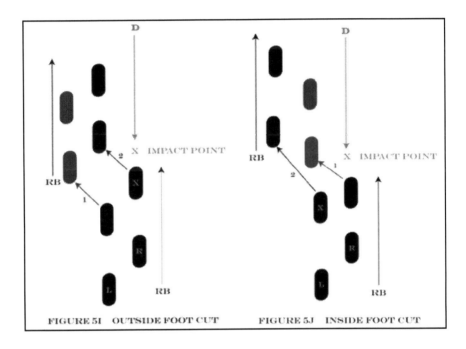

FIGURE 5I   OUTSIDE FOOT CUT   FIGURE 5J   INSIDE FOOT CUT

Cutting off of your inside foot is easier to accomplish and doesn't require as much leg strength. This technique will allow the runner to achieve a greater amount of lateral movement compared the first technique. However, timing is essential with the second technique because when you cross over your outside foot, you will briefly loose the stability of a solid base.

Understand that the defender must attack you on a centerline from his body. This is the reason why cutting, to change your angle or line of approach, is effective. In figure 5K the strike from person (d) is avoided at the point of impact (x), by the cut or side step taken by person (RB). This is because the cut placed person (RB) to the right side of the impact point (x). This same type of angular approach is used by Sil lam Kung fu artists.

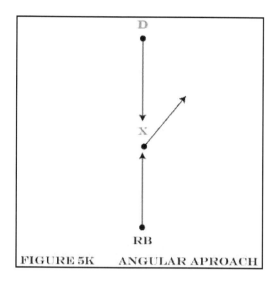

FIGURE 5K   ANGULAR APROACH

Spinning:

"Spinning" is another tool that the running back can utilize to avoid the tackle. Once again timing is crucial for the spin move to be successful. The spin must be started right before contact is made with the defender. This will cause the defender to slip off of the runner and miss the tackle.

To carry out a good spin move, start by reading the defender to determine which direction you want to spin to. Accelerate toward at the defender to make him commit to the impact. Then, just before you make contact with the defender, plant the foot that is on the same side as the direction you are spinning to. Now spin left off of the planted left foot for 180 degrees. Plant your right foot and spin for the last 180 degrees. Finally continue running down field towards the end zone. Spinning in this fashion will increase the amount of lateral movement placing you to the side of the impact point. The key is to keep your feet shoulder width apart throughout the entire spin move. This is done to help maintain good balance during the spin move. Also remember to keep the football tight against your body during the spin move. This will reduce the chance of fumbling the football. Figure 5L demonstrates the spin move.

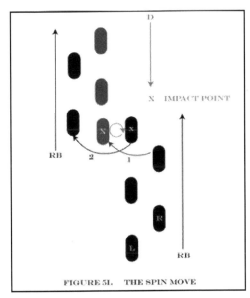

FIGURE 51.   THE SPIN MOVE

In college, I discovered that when the defender committed his momentum to the impact, I could spin in this fashion and the extra lateral movement placed me well to the side of the impact point. This would cause the defender to go flying past me taking him out of the play.

At any time if you find yourself going down to the ground, if possible, plant your free hand on the ground. Then drive your legs back underneath your upper body, recover, and keep running down field towards the end zone. This maneuver is called a "**hand plant**".

Altering speed:

A mature running back will take the hand off and, instead of sprinting full speed to the hole, he will control his acceleration to the hole. This will allow the play to develop around him. Blocks will develop and the running back will be able to read and react to them. In many cases this maturity level will make the running back more effective.

A running back that understands how pursuit angles work, will then be able to accelerate, decelerate, and change directions to avoid being tackled. This will make it harder for the defenders to choose good pursuit angles and time their impact with the running back. For example a mature running back may get the football and accelerate through the hole. Then he could possibly read the play, cut, accelerate past a defender, decelerate, read, change directions, and finally accelerate to the end zone. This unpredictability is what makes a running back devastating to the defense. Some of the best running backs of all time were masters at this.

Drills:

1. "Hand off drill":

This drill will help you master the technique of taking a hand off. Start by forming two lines 10 yards apart with one player behind the other. The front person off each line faces one another. Both lines should take one step to the right. Now the football is handed to one of the front two people. On signal both front people jog toward each other. When they pass each other the ball is handed off from person 1 into the pocket of person 2. Person 3 then starts jogging and takes the hand off from person 2 and so on. The ball should be passed to every person without being fumbled. Repetition will make the players better at taking hand offs.

Cone drills:

1. "Zigzagged cones":

This drill will help to develop your ability to avoid the tackle. Start by placing cones 10 yards apart in a zigzagged pattern. First run the cones by cutting around the outside of each one of them. Then run around the last cone and repeat this back in the direction that you came from, finishing at the starting line. Now run the cones but this time spin at each cone. Finally run the cones by doing hand plants at each cone. Once the player feels confident with the techniques he can then perform this drill while carrying the football. Repeat this drill 4 times.

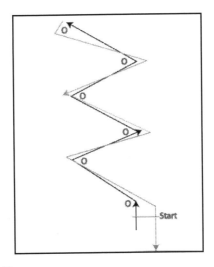

2. "Square cones":

This drill will help to develop agility and balance while changing directions. Start by placing 4 cones in a square with 5 yards between each of them. Then place the fifth cone in the center of the other cones. Now start by sprinting from cone 5 to cone 1, cut left and run to center cone 2. Stop at the center cone and then back-pedal to cone 1. Plant your feet and then shuffle sideways to cone 3. Cut and then run to center cone 2. Stop and Back-pedal to cone 3. Then sprint to cone 4, cut, and sprint through cone 5. Repeat this drill four times.

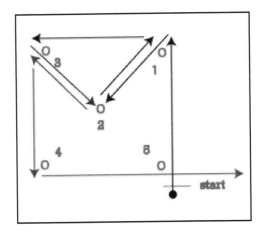

3. "Straight cones":

Place five cones on the ground in a row, with around 4 feet between them. Start by running forward to the first cone. Then cut left between the first and second cone. Next cut to the right through the second and third. Continue cutting through the cones until you pass the last cone. Shuffle left and then back pedal through the cones in the same manner. This drill will improve your agility, especially from back-pedaling through the cones. The key is to maintain a solid base and good power position throughout the drill.

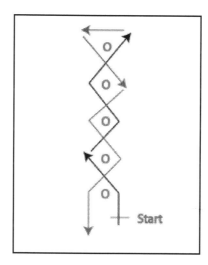

4. "Pass drills": Practice the same pass drills shown in the Receivers chapter.

CHAPTER SIX

RECEIVERS

Chapter 6: Receivers

Receivers are an important part of the offensive squad. They are vital to the offense's ability to score points. They can be used in many ways to defeat a defense. They are a quick strike force that can instantly change the momentum of the game. A good receiver core will be a valuable asset to the offensive squad.

The receiver position requires a number of attributes including agility, speed, jumping ability, vision, and good hands. A tall receiver is beneficial because, in many cases, he will be able to get higher in the air than a shorter defender. This can be an advantage allowing for a pass to be thrown above the defender. Superior speed will also make a receiver dangerous allowing him to get open for a long pass. And explosive speed will allow the receiver to create separation enabling him to catch the pass.

Form:

A good starting position should be used to maximize the receiver's ability to explode off of the line of scrimmage. First, take the proper position on the line of scrimmage. Place your feet shoulder width apart with one foot "up" and one foot "back" slightly. This will give you a runners start position maximizing your ability to explode off of the line of scrimmage. This will also allow you to go into motion easier. Bend slightly at the knees and waist. Put your hands out to the front with your elbows bent, so that you can break free from a defender if he tries to jam you. The key is to swat the defenders arms down so that he can't get ahold of you. Once contact with the defender has been broken carry out your pass route with precision. Sharp cuts and turns will make the pass route more effective. Keep in mind that you shouldn't alter your stride or look down at the ground, when you are about to cut. This is because the defender will be watching for these types of clues that will allow him to react and break on the football. Figure 6A demonstrates the starting position.

Figure 6A   The starting position

Catching the football:

Catching the football is a mandatory skill to have for this position. Using proper technique is essential to being an effective ball catcher. The receiver should strive for perfection in this area. If the receiver can touch the football with his hands, while it is in flight, then he should catch it. And he will be expected to do so.

To catch the football properly, start by placing your hands out in front of your body with the palms facing forward. Bend your elbows slightly and touch the tips of your index fingers and thumbs together. This creates a triangular space between your hands. This is where the leading tip of the football is caught. Once the football enters your hands, squeeze down on the "fat" center part of it. Then tuck the football away and run down field towards the end zone. A key thing to remember is to watch the football enter your hands, tuck it away, and then look down field for a running lane. If you take your eyes off of the football, before it is caught, you will probably miss it. So concentration is vital to succeeding at this technique. Figure 6B demonstrates the catching position.

Figure 6B The Catching Position

Blocking:

A receiver that can block a defender out, on a running play, is an asset to the team. First, to block a defender that is "playing up" right in front of you, start by exploding out of your starting stance. This should be done with the same amount of energy every time so that you do not telegraph the block. Step into the defender and extend your arms forward, placing your hands on his front numbers. Keep a solid base with your feet shoulder width apart and your knees slightly bent. Seal off the defender by placing your body between him and the ball carrier. Figure 6C demonstrates this technique.

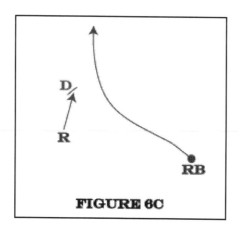

FIGURE 6C

To block a defender who is "playing back" a few yards off of the line of scrimmage, the receiver will utilize a stalk block. To carry out a stalk block, start by exploding off of the line of scrimmage. Accelerate toward the defender in the same manner that that you would to run a pass route. Close the gap on the defender. At the last moment before you pass the defender, block him out sealing him off from the ball carrier. Figure 6D demonstrates the stalk block.

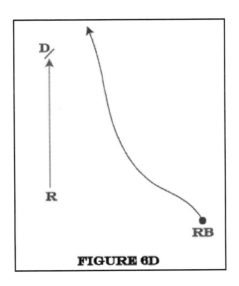

FIGURE 6D

Crack block:

In certain situations a receiver will be required to perform a "crack block". An example of this would be to seal the corner for the quarterback or a running back. To carry out an effective crack block, start by identifying the targeted defender. Do this without giving away the block. Choose the best line of travel to the impact point with the defender. Explode off of the line of scrimmage and close the gap on the targeted defender. Aim for the space between his closest shoulder and the numbers on the front of his jersey. Drive through the point of impact with the defender. You want to catch him unexpectedly so that he doesn't have time to prepare for the impact. This technique will be devastating to the defender knocking him down to the ground. Keep in mind that if

72

you can't see the defenders front numbers when you block him, you may get penalized for blocking in the back. Figure 6E demonstrates the crack block.

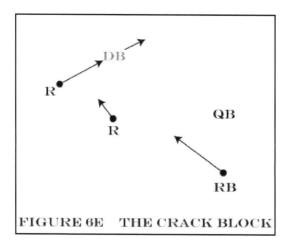

FIGURE 6E   THE CRACK BLOCK

Drills:

1. "Catching, Pole Drill":

This drill will teach you to catch the football with your hands. Find a vertical pole that is at least 6 feet tall and preferably around 3 to 4 inches wide. Start by standing directly behind the pole. Next place your arms around both sides of the pole and put your hands together in the proper ball catching position. Then tilt your head to one side so that you can see around the pole. Finally have someone throw the football to you. You will have to catch it in your hands because the pole will not allow you to use your body. Remember repetition will bring perfection.

2. "Start and Stop Drill":

This drill will improve your coordination and catching technique. This is also a good warm up drill. First walk 5 yards down field, from the quarterback, and place 2 cones 5 yards apart on the same yard line. Start at the left cone. Once the quarterback simulates the snap, run to the right cone. Then stop and turn towards the quarterback while getting into the proper catching position. The quarterback will take a 3-step drop and then pass the football to you. Catch the football and tuck it away. Then turn and sprint for 5 yards down field. Return the football to the quarterback and get back in line behind the left cone. Figure 6F demonstrates this drill. Next start by running to the right cone. Then stop, cut, and run back to the left cone. Stop and turn toward the quarter back while getting into the proper catching position. Then catch the football, tuck it away, turn and sprint 5 yards down field. Figure 6G demonstrates this drill.

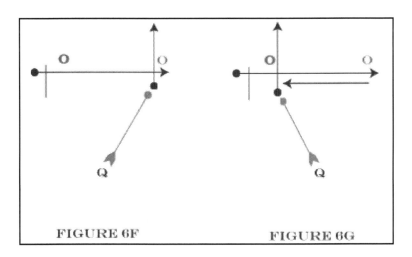

FIGURE 6F   FIGURE 6G

3. "Sideline Drill":

This drill will allow the receiver to work on catching the football over his shoulder. This drill will also allow the quarterback and the receiver to get their timing together. Start with the quarterback in the center of the field and receivers lined up towards the sideline. The quarterback snaps the ball and the receiver runs straight down field. The quarterback takes a 5-step drop and then passes the football to the receiver. The receiver looks back over the designated shoulder and locates the football in flight. He then catches the football over his shoulder and continues running down field. If the timing is right, the receiver should catch the football while running at a full sprint. He will then return the football to the quarterback and get back in line.

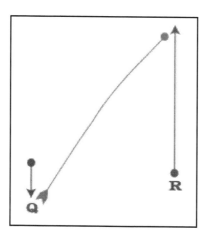

4. "Blocking Drills":

The receiver should practice proper blocking techniques. The best way to do this is with a one on one drill with a defender. Practice the blocking techniques with him playing up and playing back. The more that you practice the better you will get at blocking. Once again take pride in your ability to block a defender.

5. "Pass Routes":

The receiver should practice running pass routes with the quarterback. This will allow the receiver to master each type of rout that will be used by his team. Keep in mind that repetition will help you to perfect the route. Running pass routes will also allow the quarterback and the receivers to get their timing together. Refer to Chapter 4 (Quarterbacks), and the Drills section, to see different types of pass routes.

6. "Cone drills":

Cone drills will help the receiver increase his agility and coordination. Refer to Chapter 5 (Running backs), and the Drills section, for the different types of cone drills.

CHAPTER SEVEN

KICKERS

Chapter 7: Kickers

The kicking position is vital to the success of the team even though they rarely get recognition. This is because the team can score points by kicking a field goal successfully. So having a strong and reliable kicker should be viewed as a priority for any team.

This position requires leg strength, flexibility, explosive speed, and coordination. In many cases kickers are former soccer players. They must be athletes who can perform multiple kicking functions as well as being good tacklers. So practicing the proper tackling technique should also be considered a priority. This is because on kick offs and punts they are usually the last defender protecting the end zone from a runnning back.

Field Goals:

Field goals are an important means of scoring points. Kicking a field goal successfully requires using proper technique. The kicking motion consists of a long leg stride, a leg whip to generate foot speed, and a follow through to the target. The kickers foot speed and the point of impact on the football will translate into distance the ball travels in the air.

To kick a field goal start by taking 3 strides back and 1 stride to the side of the spot where the holder will place the football. Stand facing the impact point with your non-kicking foot forward. Then once the football is snapped step forward with your kicking foot. Then step forward to the side of the football with your non-kicking foot. This should be a long stride that will be used to generate the leg whip. Now accelerate your kicking foot through the football and follow through to the target. The top ridge of your foot should make contact just below the center part of the football. Keep your head down to look at football. Also, keep your shoulders down and square to the target. This will keep the football on line and it will keep your momentum going forward through the impact point. Figure 7A demonstrates this technique.

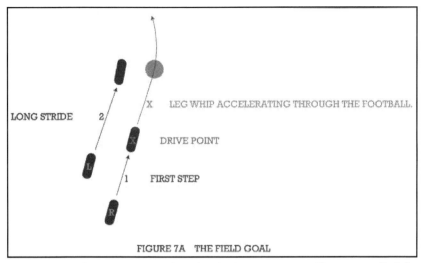

LONG STRIDE   2

X   LEG WHIP ACCELERATING THROUGH THE FOOTBALL.

DRIVE POINT

1   FIRST STEP

FIGURE 7A   THE FIELD GOAL

* Accuracy and control are both vital to succeeding as a field goal kicker.

Kick offs:

The kicker will be required to perform a variety of different types of kicking techniques for kick offs. They include the "full kick", the "squib kick", and the "onside kick". Each type of kick is designed to take advantage of weak points in the opponent's kick off return team.

The technique most often utilized by the kick off team is the "full kick". The goal of this technique is to kick the ball high in the air and long. The airtime will allow the kick off team to run down field to defend against the return. The kicker will be asked to kick the football to specific points down field. This is done to set up certain types of defensive plays. Practice kicking the football to both corners of the field and straight down the center of the field.

The next technique that will be used is the "squib kick". This technique utilizes a low line drive, while putting topspin on the football. When performed properly the ball will travel fast just above the ground. The topspin will make the ball bounce erratically off of the ground. This increases the difficulty of fielding the football and could cause a turn over. Start by placing the football on the tee. Then step back a few yards from the football to your starting position. Now stride towards the football. Take a long stride next to the football with your non-kicking foot. Then accelerate your kicking foot through the football. Kick just above the center point of the football. To get the best results, experiment by kicking on different points of the center part of the football. The ideal kick will send the football down field about 20 yards before the first bounce.

The last technique that will be used is the "onside kick". The object of this technique is to kick the football 10 yards down field in a way that your teammates can recover it. Start by placing the football on the tee in an upright position. Take the same starting position and stride towards the football. Now kick the top of the football to create topspin. The football should bounce off of the ground just in front of the tee. Then the football should travel through the air for at least 10 yards down field. The key is to get enough airtime on the football to allow your players to get under it before the opponents can catch it. Practice by kicking the football to both sides of the field. Keep in mind that if you stride towards the football in the same manner every time, it will be harder tell what type of kick is coming.

Tackling:

The kicker should practice the proper tackling technique. This is because on kick offs and punts he will be the safety valve. And his tackle could stop the return team from scoring a touch down. A kicker that is a good tackler will gain the respect of his teammates. Refer to chapter 9 (Linebackers) for the proper tackling technique.

Punting:

Punting is an important part of the kicker's duties. This is because when the offense is backed up on fourth down, the team will call for the kicker to punt the football. This is done to gain yardage before the football is turned over to the opposition. So the kicker needs to be able to punt the football for maximum effect. The speed of the punt will reduce the chance of the opposition blocking it.

To punt the football using a two-step punt, start by lining up seven yards back behind the football. If you are backed up in front of your own end zone, then this distance will be less then seven yards. Place your feet slightly less than shoulder width apart. Now check to see if your team is set, and then extend your arms forward. Put your hands together with the palms facing forward in the proper football catching position. Call for the football to be snapped. Then catch it with your hands and begin stepping forward. If you kick with the right foot then hold the football straight out horizontally over that foot. The leading tip of the football should point inward slightly. Take the first step forward with your kicking foot. Then step forward with the non-kicking foot. This should be long stride that will set up the leg whip. Then accelerate your kicking foot forward, to kick the football. The top ridge of your foot should make contact with the fat center part of the football. Now as the kicking foot accelerates upward, let the football fall straight down onto it. Drive your foot through the football and follow through, finishing up with your foot at shoulder height. Remember to watch the football leave your foot so that you do not miss kick it. Figure 7B demonstrates the punting technique.

Figure 7B   The Punting technique

CHAPTER EIGHT

DEFENSIVE LINEMEN

Chapter 8: Defensive Linemen

Defensive linemen are a crucial part of the defensive squad. They are the first line of defense protecting the end zone. They must be good run stoppers as well as good pass rushers. They should have good strength, speed, agility, size, and vision. A defensive lineman at the college level should be at least 6' 2" tall and weigh at least 250 pounds.

Defensive linemen must be aggressive and relentless in pursuing the football. This is because in many cases the quarterback will be sacked during the defensive lineman's second or third effort. He must be able to fight off the offensive lineman's block and then pursue the football. To do this the D-lineman must utilize proper form and technique. So it will be important for him to stay in balance and use the power position. Once again agility and coordination are important aspects of the defensive lineman's game.

Form:

There are a couple of different starting stances that can be utilized by the defensive lineman. They are the "three-point stance", the "four-point stance", and the "upright stance". The three-point stance is the defensive lineman's most readily used starting stance. This is because it places him in a sprinter's type starting position. The four-point starting stance is used a lot more, by defensive lineman, at lower levels of the sport. Finally, the defensive lineman can utilize the upright stance as well. But you will see this stance being used more often by blitzing linebackers.

The "upright stance" is a simple technique to perform. Start by taking your position on the line of scrimmage. Next place your feet shoulder width apart and stager them by putting one foot forward. This will give you a runner's type starting position. Bend slightly at the knees and the waist to lower your center of gravity. You should be leaning forward slightly. This will help you get off the line easier. Place your hands in a position that will allow you to defend against the block. Keep your head up so that you can see your opponent and to see where the football is. This technique will allow you to shift easier then the other techniques. Figure 8A demonstrates the upright starting stance.

Figure 8A   The Upright starting stance

The "three-point stance" is the most used of all the starting stances. This is because it provides the best position for exploding off of the line of scrimmage. The player is in an excellent driving position. This gives him the best chance to explode through the initial impact with the blocker.

To utilize the three-point stance, start by taking your position on the line of scrimmage. Next, place your feet shoulder width apart. Stager your feet to give you a runner's start position. Bend at the knees and waist and lean forward. If your left foot is forward, then place your right hand down to the ground with the tips of your fingers touching the turf. This simulates a natural running stride that will allow you to explode off of the line of scrimmage as efficiently as possible. Place your left hand on your upper left thigh in a comfortable position or straight back ready to drive forward. The heels of your feet should be turned up off of the ground slightly. This will make it possible for you to move your feet quicker. Keep your head up so that you can see where you are going and to keep your neck out of an injury prone position. When the football is snapped, explode forward by stepping forward with the rear foot and swinging the rear arm forward. This is done in the same fashion that a Track and Field sprinter explodes out of the starting blocks. Figure 8B demonstrates the three-point stance.

Figure 8B   The three-point starting stance

The "four-point stance" is a simple technique to master. Start by taking your position on the line of scrimmage. Next place your feet shoulder width apart. Then kneel down on the turf and place your hands down to the ground. The tips of your fingers and thumbs should be touching the turf. Now come up off of your knees to your hands and feet. You should be leaning forward on the toes and the balls of your feet. Then explode off of the line of scrimmage. Step off with the foot that is on the same side as you are initially moving to. Bring your hands up to the front, so that you can fight off the blocker. Figure 8C demonstrates the four-point stance.

Figure 8C   The four-point starting stance

The Bull Rush:

The "bull rush" is the base rushing technique that can be used to set up other techniques. Start by exploding off of the line of scrimmage into the blocker in front of you. Drive straight forward and extend your arms out pushing on the blocker's chest. Try to drive the blocker straight back into the quarterback by driving your legs. Extending your arms out to the front will create space between you and the blocker. This space will allow you the push off and shed the block in pursuit of the football.

A good pass rusher will use the blocker's leverage or momentum against him. To do this the defensive lineman will need to have good hand, feet, and eye coordination. Consider this, a defender is bull rushing a blocker and he has created space by extending his arms forward. Then the defender takes a step to the right. In order for the blocker to stay in front of him, the blocker will have to take a step to his left. As the blocker steps left the defender immediately pushes him in that direction and cuts back in the other direction. This will place the defender to the left side of the blocker, thus allowing the defender to move past him. The defender has just successfully used the blocker's momentum against him. Figure 8D demonstrates the Bull Rush.

Figure 8D The Bull Rush

Once you have mastered this principal, you will be able to set up the blocker for numerous pass rushing and hand techniques. They include "cut backs", "spin backs", "fore arm shivers", "arm slaps", and "swim moves".

The "cut back" and the "spin back" are both simple techniques that can be utilized to shed a blocker. To perform either technique, start by "bull-rushing" the blocker and then create space by extending your arms out to the front. Now if you want to pass the blocker on the left, then first step to the right. The blocker will step in the same direction to stay in front of you. When he does this immediately cut or spin back in the other direction, in this case to the left. If this move is timed properly it will place you to the side of the blocker allowing you to get passed him. This should be done before the blocker finishes his step, because he will not be able to shift his momentum back in the other direction. The blocker can also be pushed or nudged to the right, as you cut back to the left. Stay alert to where the football is located and relentlessly pursue it. Remember that it may take your second or third move to free you from the blocker. If you haven't freed yourself from the blocker when the pass is thrown, then put both hands up in the air in an attempt to block the football.

Balance is a critical aspect of both of these techniques. The key is to keep a solid base and to stay in the power position. Also keep in mind that if you try to cut or spin, when there is distance between you and the blocker, he will have more time to react and stay in front of you. This is why the "bull rush" is utilized to set up the other techniques.

Hand Techniques:

A hand technique is any type of technique that uses the hands to break contact with the defender. It could be made up of a number of different sequences or movements. The technique could use one hand or two hands. Some of these techniques are the 2-hand arm slap, the single hand arm slap, the swim move, forearm shivers, shoulder pulls, the shoulder punch, and the armpit punch.

To perform the "2-hand arm slap", start by bull rushing the blocker and creating space by extending your arms forward. Next bring both of your hands up above the blocker's arms. Then slap down across his arms pushing them down and to the side. If you step to the right to pass him, then slap his arms down and to the left. Figure 8E demonstrates the 2-hand arm slap.

Figure 8E

The "Single hand arm slap" is a simple technique to perform. Start by bull rushing the blocker and creating space by extending your arms forward. Then with one hand slap the defenders arms down and to the side. If you are moving to the right, then slap the defenders arms down to the left using your left hand. Figure 8F demonstrates the single hand arm slap.

Figure 8F

The "swim move" is an easy technique to master. Start by bull rushing the blocker and creating space by extending your arms forward. Next choose which direction you wish to swim to. To swim to the left, take your left hand and slap the blockers arms down to the right. Then take your right arm and rotate it up and over the blockers right shoulder while moving passed him to the left. Figure 8G demonstrates the swim move.

Figure 8G

The "forearm shiver" is an excellent technique to use to force your way passed a blocker. Start by bull rushing the blocker and creating space by extending your arms forward. Now to pass the blocker on the left, take your left hand and push the blocker's arms to the right. Then make a fist with your right hand and bring it from your right hip up to the front of your face. This is a driving motion similar to a boxer throwing an uppercut. Your right arm should drive passed the blocker's right side while you move passed him. This technique can be used to punch through the center of two blockers who are in front of you. The key is to turn your shoulders sideways when you drive the right arm in between them. This will allow you to move through the defenders by making your upper body thin. Figure 8H demonstrates the forearm shiver.

Figure 8H

The "shoulder pull" is a good technique to use to move passed a blocker. Start by bull rushing the blocker. Next to pass the blocker on the right side, take both of your hands and grab him over his left shoulder. Now pull the blocker's shoulder down and to the left while you step forward to the right. This will turn the blocker's upper body sideways taking away his leverage and power position. As a result you will be able to move passed him to pursue the football. Figure 8I demonstrates the shoulder pull. Next, try using the shoulder pull with one hand. First, use a single-hand arm slap with the outside arm. Then use the inside hand to perform a shoulder pull and move past the blocker.

Figure 8I   The Single Hand Arm Slap to Shoulder Pull

The "shoulder punch" is an effective technique for defeating a blocker who steps up to take you on. This technique should be used when you are running. Start by closing the gap on the blocker. Then aim for the blocker's shoulder on the same side that you want to pass him on. Now just before impact take both of your hands starting at your chest, extent your arms forward, and punch the palms of your hands through the targeted shoulder. This will turn the blockers upper body sideways allowing you to drive through him. Figure 8J demonstrates the shoulder punch.

Figure 8J

The "armpit punch" is an impressive technique to watch when it is performed correctly. This is because it will knock the blocker off of his feet, sending him down to the ground. Start by bull rushing the blocker and creating space by extending your arms forward. Then step to the right to force the blocker to step in the same direction. Now before the blocker can finish his step, drop your left arm down, make a fist, and bring it up and to the right catching the blocker under his armpit. This will push his upper body to the side of his center balance point, causing him to fall down on his side. Cut back to the left and close on the football. This technique will successfully use the blocker's momentum against him. And I must admit that the coolest thing I did, in my football career, was to catch another player with this technique. It didn't feel like it took a lot of effort because the timing was perfect. But to the people watching from the sidelines, the technique looked devastating. This was because it caused the other player to come off of his feet, and go falling to his side. And he would usually land on his head and one of his shoulders. Figure 8K demonstrates the armpit punch.

Figure 8K

Drills:

1. "Circle drill":

This drill will teach you how to sprint around the outside of a blocker and then come back to the quarterback. Locate or draw a circle on the ground that is about 5-yards in diameter. Place a cone at any point on the circle. This will be the starting point. Now start out in a 3-point stance. Explode off of the starting point and sprint around the outside of the circle. Once you get back to the cone, raise your arms up to simulate blocking the pass. Practice this drill in both directions.

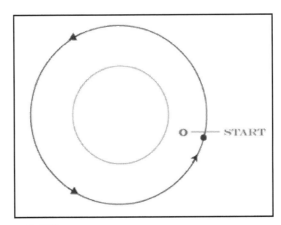

2. "One on one drill":

This drill is the best way to practice the rushing techniques that have been covered in this chapter. This drill is exactly what is says. It is one defensive lineman going up against one offensive lineman at full speed. The object is to get passed the offensive lineman and tackle the quarterback. Start by placing a tackling pad 5 yards back behind a cone. Next both players line up at the cone by getting into their starting stances. On queue explode off of the line of scrimmage and bull rush the offensive lineman. Use whatever technique it takes to beat him and get to the quarterback. Finally tackle the pad representing the quarterback. This full speed drill will improve both players' skills.

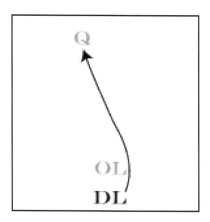

3. "Hand work drill":

This drill will help the player master the movements of the hand techniques. Start by standing facing another player. Next the other player will place his hands on your chest as if he was blocking you. Now at half speed, practice the hand techniques that were discussed in this chapter. Keep in mind that the more that you practice these techniques, the more instinctive you will perform them at full speed. This is the same reason why martial artists use repetition to learn techniques.

4. "Tackling form drill":

Start by having two players face each other one yard apart. One player will now walk through the proper tackling form. Then the other player will do this as well. Practice this while moving straight forward. Next have the opponent walk to either side and practice the tackling him from the side. But do not take your opponent to the ground in this drill. Take turns practicing this technique. This drill can now be performed at half speed. For the proper tackling technique refer to Chapter 9 (Linebackers).

CHAPTER NINE

LINEBACKERS

Linebackers

The linebackers are the defensive squad's second line of defense. They should be aggressive defenders who want to be playmakers. The linebacker should be a good run stopper, pass defender, and blitzer. So this position requires strength, speed, agility, good reactions, vision, and intelligence. A linebacker at the college level should be at least 5' 10" tall and weigh at least 210 pounds. The linebacker will often be asked to fill a leadership role.

Form:

Using proper form will allow the linebacker to move and react in the most efficient manner. He must stay in the power position to maximize his ability to take on a blocker. Even his starting stance is designed to maximize his strength and balance. So the linebacker should have an indepth understanding of balance and leverage.

Start by taking the proper position on the field. This will usually be five yards back from the line of scrimmage. Next place your feet shoulder width apart and bend slightly at the knees and waist. Your feet can be staggered by placing one foot around six inches ahead of the other. This will give you a sprinters starting position by simulating a natural running stride. Push your chest out slightly and keep your head up so that you can see down field. Now put your hands out in front of you or let them hang down to your sides. Finally, when the ball is snapped, shuffle your feet or hop slightly. This will allow you to move faster once you have read the play. In many cases martial artists will do this same thing because it will allow them to strike their target faster. Remember that if you stay in the power position and maintain the centerline balance point, you will be able to change directions easier. The key is that by staying in the power position you will maintain a lower center of gravity. This is the secret to changing directions while sprinting. Figure 9A demonstrates the starting position.

Figure 9A   The starting position

Tackling:

The linebacker must use proper technique when tackling, in order to maximize his ability to make the play. This will reduce his chance of missing the tackle. This will also reduce the chance of being injured by the contact with the ball carrier and the ground.

To tackle the ball carrier, start by identifying the best line of travel to the impact point. Then close the gap on the ball carrier while building up speed and maintaining the power position. Now lower your center of gravity to drive through the impact. Keep your head up to see the ball carrier and to keep your neck out of an injury prone position. Upon impact with the ball carrier wrap your arms around his waist, make a fist with one hand, and grip it with the other hand. Then pull your hands in towards your body to pull the ball carrier's hips forward off of his centerline. This will also push his upper body back off of the centerline. Finally, drive through the ball carrier to take him to the ground. Always keep your hands locked until the tackle is completed. Because a dangled arm can be broken apon impact with the ground. When the ball carrier is running towards the sidelines you will probably have to tackle him from the side. Do this by placing your head across the front of his body when tackling him. This will make it harder for the ball carrier to run through the tackle. Figure 9B demonstrates the proper tackling technique.

Figure 9B The Tackling Technique

Staying home:

The linebacker can make himself vulnerable, to being blocked out of the play, if he immediately flows in the direction that the play first appears to be going. This is the reason why the linebacker must "stay home" until he has read the play. To stay home a linebacker will shuffle his feet in place without moving. He will not pursue until he has determined where the football is and who is carrying it. Once the linebacker has read the play, he will then relentlessly pursue the football. By staying home the linebacker reduces the chance of being blocked out of the play, especially on cutbacks or misdirection plays. The linebacker must always stay alert because in most situations there will be an opponent assigned to block him.

Pursuit Angles:

The linebacker must understand how to utilize a good pursuit angle in order to run down a ball carrier. If you attempt to close the gap on the ball carrier from the side, you must run on an angle to the impact point not to the ball carrier. This is because by the time you get to the place where the ball carrier was at, you will end up behind him. If this happens you probably won't be able to catch him. So you must be able to judge the point downfield that you will have to get to, to intercept the ball carrier.

Linebackers

Practice and instinct will enable the linebacker to use proper pursuit angles. Figure 9C demonstrates Pursuit angles.

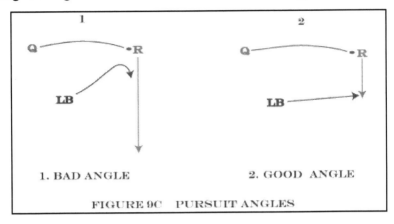

1. BAD ANGLE 2. GOOD ANGLE

FIGURE 9C PURSUIT ANGLES

Pass Drops:

The linebacker must use proper technique to effectively cover a pass play. Once he has read that the play is a pass play, he will have to drop back to guard against it. This technique can be referred to as the "pass drop".

To perform the pass drop, start by taking the proper starting position on the field. As the football is snapped, "stay home" to read the play. Once you have determined that it's a pass play, then turn your hips to the outside and run back to a predetermined point. This could be, for example, five yards back from your starting point. Call out the word "pass" to alert your teammates. Keep your head and shoulders turned towards the line of scrimmage during the pass drop. This will allow you to see if any receivers are coming into your area. It will also allow you to see the quarterback. Settle into the drop point by turning back towards the line of scrimmage. Stay in the power position because it will enable you to stop and maneuver easier. Now the quarterback will show you where he is throwing to when he releases the football. Read the angle and trajectory of the football and accelerate to the targeted receiver. Make sure that you see the football leave the quarterback's fingers, because he will sometimes use a pump fake or a shoulder turn to fake out the defenders. Relentlessly pursue the football until the play is over. Figure 9D demonstrates the pass drop.

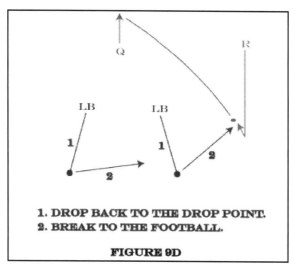

1. DROP BACK TO THE DROP POINT.
2. BREAK TO THE FOOTBALL.

FIGURE 9D

Taking on the lead blocker:

On almost all of the running plays that the linebacker will see, there will be someone assigned to block him. Strength and speed will help the linebacker avoid the block. But in many cases he will not be able to do this. So proper technique will enable him to successfully take on a blocker "straight up".

To take on the blocker "straight up", start by accelerating towards him to close the gap between the two of you. Lower your center of gravity and stay in the power position to prepare for the impact. Keep your head up so that you can see the blocker and to keep your neck out of an injury prone position. Make contact with the blocker and continue driving your legs. Now extend your arms forward to create separation between the two of you. This will allow you to push off of him to pursue the ball carrier. Finally, accelerate towards the ball carrier and tackle him using the proper tackling technique. Keep in mind that a shoulder punch can also be used to drive through the blocker. Refer to the Defensive Linemen chapter and hand techniques for the shoulder punch. Figure 9E demonstrates taking on the lead blocker.

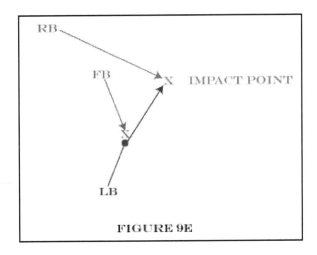

FIGURE 9E

Most coaches want to see the defender take on a blocker "straight up". This is because of the tough guy mentality of the sport. But the linebacker could easily make the blocker miss him, by taking a side step or lateral step just before the impact point. To do this start by identifying the opponent that is coming to block you. Remember that in order for him to block you, he will have to attack you on a centerline from his body. So this fact can be used against him. Make the blocker commit to the impact by running straight towards him. He will have to lower his center of gravity to prepare for the impact. Then take a side step or a lateral step just before the impact point. This will place you to the side of the impact point causing the blocker go flying passed you. Remember that if you use this technique, you must get back to the ball carrier and make the tackle, because if you don't, in many cases, the coaches will get upset and say that you shied away from contact. But I feel that this is actually an advanced skill, that when mastered, will effectively use the blocker's momentum against him. This will improve your chances of making the tackle.

Drills:

1. "Cone drills":

Cone drills are excellent drills to use to develop hand feet and eye coordination, agility, leg strength, and quickness. The linebacker should definitely use both the square cones and the straight cones drills in his training program. Refer to chapter 5 (Running backs) and the drills section for cone drills.

2. "Pursuit drill":

This drill will teach the linebackers how to use a good pursuit angle to chase down a ball carrier. It will also force the linebackers to pursue the ball carrier at a full sprint. Have a fast receiver setup by one of the sidelines. Then have the linebackers set up in the center of the field around five yards back from the line of scrimmage. Now snap the football and simulate a quick pass to the receiver who will immediately sprint straight down field. The linebackers will then pursue the receiver and touch him with at least one hand. To do this the linebackers will be forced to use good pursuit angles. Figure 9F demonstrates this technique.

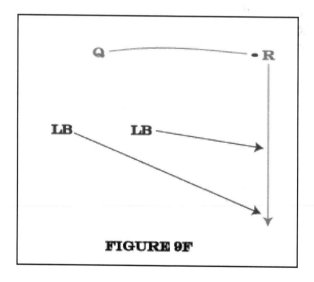

FIGURE 9F

3. "Tackling form drill":

Start by having two players face each other one yard apart. One player will now walk through the proper tackling form. Then the other player will do this as well. Practice this while moving straight forward. Next, have the opponent walk to either side of you and practice tackling him from the side, but do not take your opponent to the ground in this drill. Take turns practicing this technique. This drill can now be performed at half speed.

CHAPTER TEN

DEFENSIVE BACKS

Defensive backs are a critical part of the defensive scheme. They protect the end zone against the threat of the offense's passing game. And they must be able to step up to take on the running game. They are the last line of defense protecting the end zone.

This position requires excellent speed, agility, strength, vision, and good jumping ability. The defensive back must be able to cover a number of different types of pass routs. And he must be a great open field tackler. This is because, in many cases, he will be last defender standing between the ball carrier and the end zone. And a missed tackle could result in a touchdown.

Form:

The defensive back must utilize proper starting form when covering a pass rout. To do this, start by getting into position in front of your assigned receiver. Place your feet shoulder width apart and stagger them by placing one foot forward. This will give you a sprinters starting position by simulating a natural running stride. Bend slightly at the knees and waist to lower your center of gravity. Keep your head up so that you have a wider field of view. Let your arms hang down to your sides in a comfortable position. Figure 10A demonstrates the starting position.

Figure 10A   The starting position

Defensive backs

Technique:

Start by lining up in front of the receiver using the proper starting stance. When the receiver takes off, start back pedaling to stay in front of him. Keep your center of gravity lowered, because this will allow you to change directions easier. Glance over at quarterback to see if it is a running play or a pass play. If it is a running play then break to the football. If it is a pass play then continue covering the receiver. As the receiver sprints towards you, watch him for clues that will let you know if he is going to cut and change directions. They could be one of the following: looking down at the ground to cut, changing his running stride with short choppy steps, and lowering his hips to stop and turn around. Whatever move the receiver makes you need to be able to react to it and stay with him.

Playing up and playing back:

"Playing up" refers to the situation when the defensive back will use a starting position, in front of the receiver, at the line of scrimmage. This is done for a number of reasons including to play the run, to jam the receiver at the line of scrimmage, and to force the receiver to the outside to defend against the crossing route.

"Playing back" refers to the situation when the defensive back will use a starting position, in front of the receiver, a number of yards back off of the line of scrimmage. He will do this for a number of reasons including to combat a fast receiver, to protect against the deep pass, and to set up zone coverage.

Covering the stop route:

The stop route consists of the receiver sprinting straight down field to a predetermined point. He will then instantly stop and turn back towards the quarterback to catch the pass. It could be a five-yard stop route, a ten-yard stop route, or any other distance.

Defensive backs

To cover the "stop route", start by lining up in front of the receiver using the proper starting technique. Once the football is snapped, start backpedaling if you are playing back. If you are playing up, then jam the receiver off of the line to force him to the outside, and then rotate your hips and sprint along side of his inside hip. Now watch the receiver for clues that will give away his next move. Remember to glance at the quarterback periodically to see where the ball is. Once the receiver stops and turns around, plant your feet and cut back to him while looking for the football. Remember to stay in the power position so that you can change directions, in the event that the receiver takes off again. If the football is in flight, then extent your inside arm across the front of the receiver in an attempt to block the pass. Place your outside arm behind the receiver to put yourself into position to make the tackle, in the event that you miss the block. Your timing is crucial because if you make contact with the receiver, before the football is touched, then you will be called for a penalty. Figure 10B demonstrates this technique.

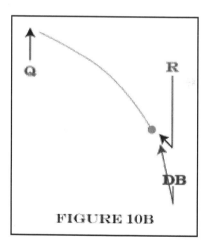

FIGURE 10B

Covering the Fly route:

The fly route is probably the most remembered pass route. This is because of the speed and length of the pass route which in many cases results in a touchdown. It has been called many names including the fly route, the bomb, and the go route. It can be an exciting play to watch, and it can be a momentum shifter for that team.

To cover the "fly route", start by lining up in front of the receiver utilizing the proper starting position. Jam the receiver off of the line of scrimmage to force him to the outside if you are playing up. Rotate your hips to the outside and begin running by the inside hip of the receiver. If you are playing back, then start backpedaling when the receiver takes off of the line of scrimmage. Once the receiver closes on you, then rotate your hips to the outside and run forward along his inside hip. Glance at the quarterback to see where the football is. Now use the sideline to your advantage by forcing the receiver towards it to reduce his operational space. Do this by running on an angle towards the sideline. Glance back again briefly to look for the football. Keep reading the receiver's body to determine if he is about to catch the football. Then once he reaches to catch the football, extend your inside arm across his arms in an attempt to block it. Extend your outside arm around the back of the receiver's waist. This will put you into position to wrap up the receiver and make the tackle, if he catches the football. Try to push the receiver out of bounds before he can place both of his feet on the ground, because this will result in the play being ruled an incomplete pass. Figure 10C demonstrates this technique.

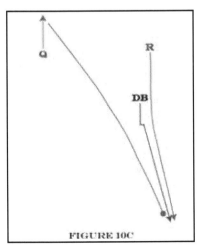

FIGURE 10C

Stripping the football:

The defensive back can utilize a few techniques to strip the football. This is done for the sole purpose of causing a turnover. These techniques are the overhand strip and the underhand strip. Both techniques are simple to master. And the ability to strip the football is a skill that the defensive back must have in his arsenal.

To perform the "overhand strip" start by closing the gap on the ball carrier. Now if you are on his right side, then put your left arm across his back to grip his left shoulder. Then bring your right arm down across the football in an attempt to knock it out of his hands. This motion is similar to the hammer fist strike used by martial artists. If this doesn't work then grip the football with your right hand and try to rip it back towards your body. Figure 10D demonstrates the overhand strip.

Figure 10D The Overhand Strip

To perform the "underhand strip", start by closing the gap on the ball carrier. Now if you are on his right side, then extend your left hand around his back to grab his left shoulder. Then take your right arm and bring it up through the bottom of football, in an attempt to strip it. This motion is similar to the natural upward swing of the arm, during sprinting. Figure 10E demonstrates this technique.

Figure 10E The Underhand Strip

Breaking on the football:

A defensive back that is skilled at breaking on the football will be an immediate threat to the offense. This is because of his ability to intercept the pass and score a touchdown. If the defensive back does break on the football, he must either catch it or knock it down to the ground. If he doesn't do this, the receiver could catch the football and he will be out of position to make the tackle.

To break on the football, start by lining up in front of the receiver using the proper starting technique. When the receiver takes off of the line of scrimmage, start backpedaling. Glance at the quarterback to see where the football is. Watch for the subtle hints that will let you know if the receiver is about to cut or stop. React to his move when he makes it. Glance at the quarterback to read where he is throwing the football. Determine the angle and trajectory of the football and break to the point where you can catch it. In many cases this will put you just in front of the receiver, thus catching the pass before he can. Finally accelerate down field towards the end zone. Figure 10F demonstrates this technique.

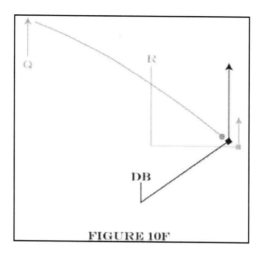

FIGURE 10F

Man-to-man and Zone coverage:

There are two basic types of coverage strategies used by the defensive squad. They are the man-to-man coverage and the zone coverage. Both techniques have their strengths and weaknesses. The defense will alternate between each technique in an attempt to match up with the offense. These techniques will largely affect the way that the defensive backs operate during the play.

Man-to-man coverage is basically what it states. Each defensive back will be assigned a specific receiver to cover. The defensive back will mirror that receiver wherever he goes, in an attempt to protect against the pass. This technique will be most effective when the defender is matched up with a receiver in an attempt to neutralize his abilities. For example if the receiver is faster then the defensive back, than this is a bad match up. This is because the receiver will be able to use his speed to burn the defensive back on a long pass.

Zone coverage consists of breaking up the defensive side of the field into sections or zones. Then each zone will be assigned to a defensive player who will settle into it and defend it. The defensive back will be responsible for covering passes in his zone. Once the quarterback passes the football, the defensive backs can then leave their zones and relentlessly pursue the football.

Defensive backs

Drills:

1. "Tackling form drill":

Start with two players standing across from each other around one yard apart. One player will now walk through the proper tackling form, using the other player as the tackling dummy. But he should not take the other player down to the ground. Now have the other player walk to either side and practice the proper tackling technique from the side. Refer to Chapter 9 (Linebackers) for the proper tackling technique.

2. "Back pedal drill":

This drill will teach the player to run backwards at full speed while maintaining a good power position. Start by taking the proper starting stance. Now start backpedaling while maintaining proper form. Stay in balance and keep a low center of gravity. Backpedal for twenty yards and then get back in line.

3. "Backpedal cut drill":

This drill will help you turn and change directions while running backwards. Start by placing four cones ten yards apart in a zigzagged pattern. Line up on the first cone and start backpedaling towards the second cone. When you get to the second cone plant your feet, rotate your hips, and backpedal towards the third cone. Once you reach the third cone rotate your hips and start backpedaling towards the fourth cone. Then when you reach the fourth cone rotate your hips and switch to running forward. Finally, sprint forward for another five yards.

4. "Pursuit drills":

This drill will teach the defensive backs to use proper pursuit angles and run at full speed. Refer to Chapter 9 (Linebackers) and the drills section for pursuit drills.

5. "Cone drills":

Cone drills will help the defensive back develop agility and coordination. Refer to Chapter 5 (Running backs) and the drills section for cone drill.

6. "Ball catching drills":

A defensive back that can catch the football is dangerous offering the threat of the interception. The defensive back should work on his ability to catch the football. Refer to chapter 6 (Receivers) and the drills section for ball catching drills.

CHAPTER ELEVEN

TECHNICAL SUBJECTS

Mental Toughness:

Mental toughness is a key ingredient in excelling at a highly competitive and physical sport like football. Mental toughness can be defined as a state of mind that produces a heightened tolerance level to physical and mental strains. This state of mind can be developed through numerous processes including adversity, hardship, and extremely rigorous physical training. I feel that every person can achieve a higher level of mental toughness through physical training and hardship.

Mental toughness will allow the player to keep driving or fighting until his mission is accomplished. I refer to this as "being able to play outside the limits of your body". When I played football in college, I would get "contusions" or extreme bruising all over my body. My teammates would say, " Dam you got beat up". But the reality of the situation was that I caused the bruising to myself by playing outside the limits of my body. Mental toughness will allow you to keep coming or keep fighting passed the point where you would normally quit or give up.

Mental toughness will give you another tool to excel and win while playing a sport. When I play a sport, "I play to win. And I want to win with perfection." So when I played football, I wanted to beat my competitor every play. I would never quit, or never stop coming, until I whooped that player, every play. As a result my teammates would refer to me as a machine. And this was a direct result of my mental toughness.

The foundations of my mental toughness were developed through hardships during my youth. I achieved a heightened level of mental toughness during the four years I spent in the US Army's 82nd Airborne Division. This was the key ingredient that allowed me to train harder then the rest. So I trained for football all year long, at least four days a week.

Strength training:

"Strength training" is an essential aspect of excelling at a contact sport. It will help you become more competitive and it will allow you to withstand impacts without sustaining injuries. It is also an important ingredient in developing explosive speed. So if you are considering the pursuit of a contact sport, then you should to look into starting a strength training program.

There are two types of lifts that make up a strength training regimen. They are the main lift and the accessory lift. The main lift is an exercise that uses a number of different muscle groups to accomplish it. The main lifts are the parallel squat, the bench press, the dead lift, and the power clean. The main lift will partially tear down a number of different muscle groups. Accessories are lifts that isolate on specific muscles or muscle groups. They are used to complete the tear down process for that muscle or muscle group.

In strength training, proper form and technique will have positive effects on the player. Proper form will reduce the risk of injury by reducing the amount of pressure being placed on the joints. This will allow the player to use heavier weight to develop muscle mass. Proper technique will increase the effectiveness of the workout. This is accomplished by increasing the amount of isolation on the targeted muscle group. For example, if a player trains using two different techniques for a specific time period. The technique that isolates the best, on the targeted muscle group, will result in the most gains. The object is to increase your strength level over the full range of motion of that muscle group.

There are a number of different types of muscle fibers. A couple of the fiber types are important to the athlete's ability to play contact sports. They are the red cell and the white cell. These types of muscle fibers will determine the player's level of strength and fast twitch or explosive speed. A certified personal trainer can help you develop training programs to target them. The training program should be designed to develop strength, explosive speed, and muscle endurance.

Nutrition also plays a part in the development of the muscle mass. This is because the human body uses proteins and amino acids to build and repair muscle tissue. When the athlete trains hard and regularly, he will have to take in allot of nourishment to gain or maintain his muscle mass. In many cases he will not get all of the nutrition that he needs from eating food. This is why it is beneficial for the player to take nutritional supplements. So nutrition is also an important part of the player's training program. A certified nutritionist can help the player design a nutrition program to go along with his training program.

* The following is an **Off-season strength training program** that I used in my football career. Always consult a physician before starting a training program.

1. Monday: Heavy day

Warm up and stretch.

Parallel Squat: 4 sets X 6 repetitions = increasing weight for
each set.
1 down set X 10 reps. = 60 pounds less than the
heaviest set.

Bench Press: 4 sets X 6 reps. = increasing weight for each set.
1 down set X 10 reps. = 60 pounds less than the
heaviest set.

Stiff Legged dead lift: 3 sets X 10 reps. = increasing weight for
each set.

Power clean: 3 sets X 10 reps. = increasing weight for each set.

Accessories: 3 sets X 8 reps = for each of the accessories that
you do.

2. Friday: Light day

Warm up and stretch.

Parallel Squat: 4 sets X 15 reps. = use medium to light weight.

Bench press: 4 sets X 15 reps. = use medium to light weight.

Stiff legged dead lift: 3 sets X 15 reps = use medium to light weight.

Power clean: 3 sets X 15 reps. = use medium to light weight.

Accessories: 2 sets X 15 reps = use medium to light weight. Do this for each of the accessories that you do.

*Repeat this program weekly.

The Parallel Squat:

Remember that it is important to increase your strength level over the full range of motion. This is because during a "straight up" impact with an opponent, the player will be in a running stride. This means that he will be bent at the knees and waist. So if he doesn't increase his strength over the lower end of the squat motion, he will probable loose the impact with the other player. Another words if he can only squat 300 pounds at the lower half of the squat motion and the other player can squat 500 pounds at the lower half of the squat motion. Then he will be over powered and loose the impact. The squat is parallel when the top edge of the knee joint is parallel to the top edge of the hip joint. You should be able draw a horizontal line from the knee joint to the hip joint.

Proper form will enable the player to train with heavier weight without putting pressure on his joints. This will decrease the chance being injured during squatting. Start by gripping the bar with your fingers over the top and the thumbs underneath. Place your index fingers over the 2 lines cut into the bar. This will ensure that the bar is centered on your back. The bar should sit on your back in the natural groove between the top backside of the shoulder muscles and the base of the trap muscles. Step back with the bar and set you feet around a foot wider than shoulder width apart. This is referred to as the "sumo squat". Your feet should point outward slightly to maintain the proper knee and ankle joint alignment. Take a deep breath and then start the motion by rotating your hips backwards and squatting down to the parallel point. Push your chest out slightly and look up and to the front. This will keep you from leaning forward and doing a nosedive. You should be able to draw vertical lines from the ankle joints to the knee joints. If the knees move forward in front of the vertical lines, then pressure will be transferred to the knee joints. And this pressure could cause injuries to the knee joints. Now explode upward and rotate your hips back under the bar. Exhale as you drive upward. You should finish up back in the starting position. Remember the goal is to increase your strength over the full range of motion. In figure 11A, I demonstrate the parallel squat with 410 pounds. 620 pounds is my personal best.

A. The Starting position.   B. The parallel position.

C. Exploding upward.   D. Finishing at the starting position.
Figure 11A The parallel squat

The Bench Press:

The bench press will develop the power needed to drive your arms forward into an opponent. This power is crucial to the player's ability to block, push off of an opponent, and utilize hand techniques. Once again it is important for the player to increase his strength levels over the full range of motion. This will ensure that he has the ability to overpower his opponent in close and with created separation.

It is important for the player to utilize proper form and technique when performing the bench press. This will help reduce the chance of sustaining injuries while bench pressing. This is because it will reduce the amount of pressure being placed on the joints. It will also increase the amount of isolation on the muscle groups. And the player will be able to use heavier weight to develop muscle mass.

To perform the bench press, start by sitting down on the end of the bench. Place your feet flat on the ground shoulder width apart. The feet should point outward slightly to maintain proper knee and ankle joint alignment. You should be able to draw vertical lines from the ankle joints to the knee joints. Once your feet and buttocks are set they should not be moved until the lift is completed. Next lay back on the bench without hitting your head on the weight bar. Grip the bar by placing the same fingers of each hand on the lines cut into it. I place my pinkie fingers on the lines. Grip the bar by wrapping your fingers around the top and wrapping your thumbs around the bottom of it. Always wrap your thumbs around the bar because they will stop it from rolling out of your hands and falling down onto your chest. Arch your back slightly and tighten up the muscles in your legs. This will transfer leverage to your upper body. Keep in mind that once you are set, your feet, buttocks, shoulders, and head should not move and should remain touching the floor and the bench. Next, lift the bar out of the racks. The bar should start out straight above your shoulder joints. Take a deep breath and then lower the bar to your chest in a controlled manner. The bar should touch your body across the base of your chest muscles. You should be able to draw a vertical line from your elbow joints to your wrist joints. Now drive the bar upward returning it to the starting position. And remember to exhale as you drive the bar upward. In figure 11B, I demonstrate the bench press with 320 pounds. 450 pounds is my personal best.

A. The starting position.   B. The bottom resting position.

C. Exploding Upward.   D. Finishing at the starting position.
Figure 11B   The bench press.

In Season and Off Season training:

A one-year period can be broken up into two training regimens. They are the In Season regimen and the Off Season regimen. The In Season regimen is designed to maintain the gains that were achieved during the off-season. And the Off Season regimen is designed to increase the player's abilities for the next football season.

Many players will relax or slack off during the off-season. This is a big mistake because the off-season makes up the largest portion of the year. The off-season will allow all of your nagging injuries to heal, from the football season. This is the best time to increase your speed, agility, strength, explosiveness, and technical skills.

The player should set goals that he wants to accomplish during the off-season. The goals should be written down in a notebook. The notebook should also be used to record information from training sessions. This should include body weight, exercises performed, how the player felt, weak points that need to be improved, injuries and treatments. This information will be extremely valuable in assessing progress and training regimen effectiveness.

You should be able to start each season in a better position than the last year. This means that you should have increased your muscle mass, dropped tenths of a second off of your forty-yard dash time, added inches to your vertical leap, increased your explosiveness, become more agile (better foot work), and improved your basic techniques. The off-season is the time when the gains are made through hard work and dedication.

* The following is an example of **goals** that can be set for the off-season:

Increase speed: Drop 2 tenths of a second off of 40 yd. Dash time.

Increase vertical leap: 2 inches.

Increase body weight: achieve 230 lbs. at 10 % body fat, a 10 lb. increase.

Improve agility: take martial arts and perform agility drills.

Improve ball catching: perform drills and concentration work.

Increase strength: achieve main lifts max. weight increases of 35 lbs.

The off-season can now be broken up into weekly intervals with set workout sessions for each day. The player must evaluate himself every couple of weeks to determine if the training regimen is getting results. Remember that it is easy to work on the things that you are good at. But you must also identify the things that you weak at and work hard on improving them as well. The key is to keep improving your game every year.

* The following is an example of a **Weekly off-season training program.**

Week 1:

1. Monday: Strength training heavy day

2. Tuesday: Sprints and agility drills

3. Wednesday: Recovery day, no workout

4. Thursday: Plyometrics or Strength shoes training

5. Friday: Strength training light day

6. Saturday: Light sprints and technical work

7. Sunday: Recovery day, no workout

During the in-season your timing and techniques will come together. The goal of this time period is to maintain the gains that have been made during the off-season. The player should perform a heavy day strength training session early in the week. The rest of the week will be taken up by team practices, in preparation for the football game that week. When I played college football, I would lift weights on Mondays during the season. This was because it would allow my muscles to recuperate by the football game on Saturday. And by lifting weights I would be able to maintain my strength levels.

* The following is an example of my **In-season strength training workout:**

Monday, Heavy day

1. Parallel Squat: 4 sets X 8 reps. = increasing weight
    (I would squat 405 lbs. X 8 reps. for the heavy set.)

2. Bench press: 4 sets X 8 reps. = increasing weight
    (I would bench 315 lbs. X 8 reps. for the heavy set.)

3. Power clean: 4 sets X 8 reps. = increasing weight
    (I would power clean 225 lbs. X 8 reps.)

4. Stiff leg dead lift: 4 sets X 8 reps. = increasing weight

5. Accessories: 2 sets X 8 reps. = for each accessory
    performed

Passion:

How many times have you heard the saying "For the love of the game"? This saying is a critical aspect of achieving success in whatever you are undertaking. This is because if you love what you are doing, you will become passionate about it. Passion will drive you to become successful at that thing, in this case a sport. Passion will also bring a level of boundless energy toward pursuing that sport.

I remember when I was young all that I wanted to do was to play sports. And if I wasn't eating or sleeping I was playing sports. I could play sports all day long back then and I never got tired of it. Even to this day, I still long for time when I can play sports. And sports still consume my thoughts and dreams.

Technical subjects

Being passionate about something will help you achieve childhood levels of energy. If you love it, you will be successful at it, and it will bring you happiness. Discover what you are passionate about, what your dreams are, and pursue them with childhood energy.

Acknowledgements:

Special thanks to the Amity Vikings, mights and midgets football team in Berks county Pennsylvania. This was where I was first introduced to the game of football. And I was hooked.

Special thanks to the E.L.C.O. high school football coaches. During this time in my career, I learned basic skills and techniques of the game. And I also increased my love for the game.

Special thanks to Head coach Jim Sypult, coach Bob Swank, and the Methodist College Monarchs, for giving me the opportunity to play college football and receive a quality education. It was during this time in my career that I gained an extensive understanding of the game of football and its techniques. During this time, I also had the opportunity to test and prove the effectiveness of techniques that I thought up. It was great to be a part of a winning tradition.

Special thanks to Head coach Dedrick Wise and the Norfolk Nighthawks (AF2 league), for giving me the opportunity to sign a players contract for the 2001 season. It was during training camp and the early part of the season that I picked up advanced techniques and skills of the game, through observation.

Special thanks to the Winning Factor Personal Training Center and John Schaeffer (my father), for teaching me about strength training and sports conditioning. I learned extensively about strength training through instruction and application of the principals, over a 10 year period.

Special thanks to Harold "buzz" Putt for his friendship and support of my trials and endeavors.

Special thanks to Tony Tallis and the South Mountain Fitness Center, for allowing me to use their facilities to film the squat and bench techniques.

My Thoughts:

"Drive"

By, Jeff Schaeffer

A bitter taste, from brief success.
So I can see that I am not there yet.
Imperfection, yet another lesson.

I must work harder than ever before.
So I give it my all, until I fall to the floor.

Again and again they stare at me.
They don't understand what's driving me.

My vision is clear and all I see.
Is that when I'm the best!
I will finally be free.
Drive.

My Thoughts:

"Focus"

By, Jeff Schaeffer

My visions are clouded.
Indecision, obstruction.

I lye in bed to pass the time.
Squinting, blinking.
No notice, come on focus.

Where did it go, that incredible desire.
To accomplish the tasks of an inner fire.

What was burning was plain to see.
But now I can't even feel the heat.
So what is life with nothing to do.

It's the morning light and the day is new.
So I look out the window to take in the view.
The sky begins to clear and I discover something cruel.
It's that one man's survival depends on the fuel.
Focus.

ISBN 141200512-4

9 781412 005128

26342457R00077

Made in the USA
Lexington, KY
22 December 2018